The MOUNTAIN of the LORD

Other books by Chad S. Hawkins

The First 100 Temples
Holy Places: True Stories of Faith and Miracles from Latter-day Temples
Latter-day Heroes
Youth and the Temple: What You Want to Know and How You Can Prepare
Faith in the Service: Inspirational Stories from LDS Servicemen and Servicewomen

The MOUNTAIN *of the* LORD

TRUE STORIES
OF FAITH AND MIRACLES FROM
LATTER-DAY TEMPLES

written and illustrated by
CHAD S. HAWKINS

DESERET
BOOK

SALT LAKE CITY, UTAH

The images of temples included in this volume are available as fine art prints from Deseret Book Company and other distributors of LDS products. For more information, contact Chad Hawkins Art, Inc., by telephone at 801-544-3434; by FAX at 801-544-4122; by mail at P. O. Box 292, Layton, UT 84041; or by e-mail at artist@integrity.com.

If you have documented stories regarding temples in your area that you would like to share, please e-mail them to the author at artist@integrity.com.

Illustrated endsheets of Solomon's Temple by Chad S. Hawkins.

Library of Congress Cataloging-in-Publication Data

Hawkins, Chad S., 1971–
    The mountain of the Lord : true stories of faith and miracles from latter-day temples / written and illustrated by Chad S. Hawkins.
        p. cm.
    Includes bibliographical references and index.
    ISBN 978–1–60641–633–4 (hardbound : alk. paper)
    1. Mormon temples—History.   2. Mormon temples—Anecdotes.   3. Mormon temples—Pictorial works.
I. Title.
    BX8643.T4H387 2010
    246'.95893—dc22   2009052498

Printed in the United States of America
Worzalla, Stevens Point, WI

10   9   8   7   6   5   4   3   2   1

Für Stephanie,
Die Liebe meines Lebens,
die Mutter von unseren fünf Kindern

CONTENTS

CONTENTS

CONTENTS

CONTENTS

ACKNOWLEDGMENTS

I would like to thank all those who made this book possible. I give credit and appreciation to those who are represented in this book through their stories. Their wonderful experiences concerning the temple bless and strengthen all of us. I would also like to offer my heartfelt appreciation to Sheri Dew and Jana Erickson of Deseret Book. Thanks also to my editor, Leslie Stitt, and to Shauna Gibby and Tonya Facemyer of the Deseret Book publication team. And last but not least, I am grateful to my wife and children for their continued love and support.

INTRODUCTION

I like to go running. To lace up my shoes and disappear down the road is, for me, one of life's sweetest pleasures. Whenever I travel, my running shoes go with me. My shoes and I have put in some long miles in historic and picturesque locations around the world.

When I attended the Hill Cumorah Pageant in Palmyra one year, I ran most mornings on a pathway located a few feet away from the historic Erie Canal. With every stride, I thought of the famous waterway's impact on that region as well as on Church history. One morning, my run took me along Stafford Road and finally down the middle of what used to be the Smith family farm property. As I approached the Smith property, I stopped running. I knew I was treading upon sacred ground. I soon was standing in a position where I could see the Sacred Grove on one side and the Palmyra New York Temple on the other. I pondered how exciting it is to live in this era of Church history. To live in a day when the gospel of Jesus Christ has been restored and to also witness an era of temples dotting the earth is truly a choice blessing.

I had similar feelings when visiting another historic latter-day temple. During the Nauvoo Illinois Temple open house, I had the opportunity one evening to be among those cleaning the temple. I recorded in my journal: "Today I had an experience of a lifetime. I was able to clean the Nauvoo Temple in preparation for the next day's open house tours. I was given the assignment to wipe down the hardwood flooring on the spiral staircase! I loved to polish the handrails because they were so perfectly crafted." After completing our tasks, those in the cleaning crew were given a thorough tour of the temple. I was continually amazed at the attention to historic detail. When I was in the celestial room I noticed the white antique doorstops—a tiny, maybe insignificant detail, but true to the pioneer era. On the top floor, we entered a room that enabled us to ascend into the spire. At the very top, I looked through the small pieces of glass onto the roof of the temple, over old Nauvoo, and out west beyond the mighty Mississippi. I was told that the glass through which I was looking was among the many pieces of hand-blown glass used on the temple. From the ground, no one would ever be able to discern that the small glass panels in the tower were hand-blown glass with its unique texture. Yet, even in this most inconspicuous place, genuine care was given.

Those who labored to build the Nauvoo Illinois Temple demonstrated their dedication to the Lord's house by offering the best of their trades and abilities. Many more from around the world demonstrate a similar dedication by faithful temple service. Such dedication was demonstrated by a brother I met named Alexander Diloyan. I was in Sweden attending the Stockholm Temple in preparation for an upcoming painting. Following my stay in Sweden, I was planning on traveling to the Helsinki Finland Temple open house. My flight plans from Stockholm to Helsinki took me though Latvia. It was on my flight from

Stockholm to Latvia that I had the pleasure of becoming acquainted with Brother Diloyan. He and his wife were converted to the gospel while living in the Ukraine. Six years later, they were called to serve temple missions in Stockholm. They accepted the call and served faithfully for two years, at great personal and financial sacrifice. When I met them, they were heading back to a struggling land where they would have to rebuild their lives. As he was literally flying back to an existence of uncertainty, he said to me, "The last two years of serving in the temple have been the best two years of my life. There is nothing I would change about serving in the temple." I am a better person for having met Brother Diloyan, and I will never forget his example.

As I developed the concept of this publication, I gave specific attention to the book's design and layout. The idea for this book's square shape came from Dave Martin, who served as the historian for the Columbus Ohio Temple. He designed the beautiful two-hundred-page historical book about the temple's construction to be square in shape. Following his example, I chose this symbolic shape for this book and two previous publications, *Holy Places: True Stories of Faith and Miracles from Latter-day Temples* and *Gift of Love: The Houston Texas Temple*.

As with all the publications I have authored, I have given my best effort to document and write historical events pertaining to the holy temple in the most accurate and reverent manner. I have, whenever possible, made an exhaustive effort to find multiple credible sources for each story and to be true to a strict standard of conveying the facts without aggrandizement. None of the material in this book was used without express permission or without being previously published.

Since the days of the first temple in this dispensation, miracles and stories of sacrifice and faith have been associated with all aspects of temple work. The same is true today. These special and sacred events remind us that this is the Lord's work, and it is our privilege to be a part of it. This book contains many inspiring and miraculous events. For every one of these, however, there are thousands of others that occur quietly among the faithful, temple-loving members of the Church. The temple has a way of refining our spiritual senses as we live our lives in a temporal world. I was taught an important truth by the first president of the Lubbock Texas Temple, Jay B. Jensen. He shared this insight during one of our conversations: "I receive inspiration in the temple not because I am the temple president. I receive inspiration because I am *in* the temple."

A Church official who had responsibilities in the Eastern Europe Area region once told me that in order for a stake of Zion to be spiritually mature, it needs to have access to a temple. As I pondered his comment, I thought that, likewise: for us to make progress and develop spiritually, we need to be utilizing our access to the temple. It is a testimony to me that the temple is truly a special and eternal edifice. Those who choose to make the temple a focus in their lives will be blessed daily by having an enriched perspective of our Savior's divine purpose.

EXPEDITION OF FAITH

Accra Ghana Temple

Sierra Leone, located on the west coast of Africa, has been a fertile location for Church growth since the first branch was organized in 1988. In a region laden with violence and political uncertainty, Church members found strength and hope in the restored gospel of Jesus Christ. Despite numerous challenges, including war, poverty, and isolation, Church membership grew to over five thousand at the time of the Accra Temple dedication in January 2004.

Two years later, in October 2006, a group of forty faithful members accompanied by their children made a trip to the temple. It took months of saving and planning. The travelers rode in a non-air-conditioned bus, sitting on hard benches. To save space, children sat on their parents' laps for the entire trip. Due to violent civil war, they chose not to take a direct route through the country of Ivory Coast. Instead they traveled through three neighboring countries, which added six hundred miles and three days to their journey.

For some members, the expense of the journey was the equivalent of six months' earned wages. Some making the journey had to negotiate with their employers so they wouldn't lose their jobs. All were responsible for their own provisions, which consisted mainly of bananas, pineapple, cassava, papaya, and breads. Not knowing their trip would take so long, many ran out of food and water on the third day. Since the meager amount of Sierra Leone currency they brought with them was not accepted in the countries through which they traveled, most were unable to purchase vital necessities along the way. During one roadside family home evening, Bo Sierra Leone district president Solomon Khan likened their trip to that of the pioneers crossing the plains, who also ran short of food or water.

After traveling 113 hours, the weary travelers arrived at the beautifully lit temple at three in the morning. With tears in their eyes and while still in the bus, they bowed their heads and offered a prayer of thanks to their Heavenly Father for the safe journey.

After receiving food and water, their next priority was to wash the road dust off of their clothes. Most had only their clothes for the temple and those that they wore on the bus. Unaccustomed to using washers and dryers, which are located in a building next to the temple, these humble members started to wash their clothes in the room's wash basin. The members were joyful to be taught how to use the machines by public affairs director Thane Hales.

During the three days they were at the temple, from the time the temple opened until the time it closed, these Saints served in every session, and the adult members all received their long-awaited endowments and sealings. Ghana Accra mission president Robert Gay and his wife, Lynette Gay, provided food for these Saints for their trip home, and they began their long journey home rejoicing at their opportunity to finally serve in the Lord's house.[1]

The speed and efficiency of the Accra Temple's construction was noticed by the casual passersby, city leaders, and political officials. Six months prior to the temple's dedication, Mary Cartin Yates, the U.S. ambassador to Ghana, toured the construction site, accompanied by Elder Sheldon F. Child of the Seventy and president of the Africa West Area. The ambassador commented that she had "never seen anything so complex go up so quickly here in Ghana."[2]

TIMELESS AND SACRED GROUND

Stockholm Sweden Temple

The Stockholm Sweden Temple is built in the forested community of Haninge. Archaeologists believe the area where the temple stands has been inhabited since the Hunter Stone Age (5000 BC). Proof of habitation from the Bronze Age and the Iron Age to the present day has been carefully excavated and researched. It is estimated that around 360 generations have lived on the grounds around the temple.

Construction on the temple was delayed for three years while an excavation of the site was performed. Seventeen graves of different sizes were found, although not all were excavated. For that reason, certain areas of the temple grounds cannot be altered. The oldest grave dates back to around 700 BC. It was positioned on the ground's highest point, exactly where the temple now stands. Because of its strategic location, it is believed to have belonged to a person of prominence.

An additional discovery was made just outside the temple grounds in the year 2000. As a housing development began, the remains of an ancient heathen temple dating between 400 BC and AD 400 were unearthed. The only one known of its kind in Sweden or northern Europe, this sensational find, which is similar to the ancient temples found in Rome or Greece, was given extensive media coverage. Since the distance between the old and new temples is only fifty-five yards, the public road that runs between the two temple sites was named Templevägen (Temple Street) by the community. The LDS temple location has the respect of the entire nation and was visited by the king and queen of Sweden on 23 August 1995.

In the early 1980s, there were several attractive locations upon which the temple could have been built. However, members feel that it was the hand of the Lord that brought together the past and the present at this peaceful location. It is interesting that a temple, whose purpose is to bring salvation to the deceased, is itself situated among gravesites. The blessed feeling that comes from visiting this holy temple provides deeper meaning to the concept of turning the hearts of the children to their fathers.[1]

The Kirtland Temple and the Stockholm Sweden Temple share a common architectural design. Found on the tower of the Kirtland Temple is a wooden decorative circle with four keystones, located at the primary north, south, east, and west locations. This same element is repeated on the Stockholm Temple. The temple's freestanding, square spire base is adorned with this circle and keystone design. They are positioned on each of its four sides and glisten with gold color. Several of the windows of the temple are also created in this beautiful design.

THE HOTTEST TICKET ON BROADWAY

Manhattan New York Temple

As the Manhattan New York Temple neared completion, mounting anticipation for the public open house increased. Church officials carefully considered their methods of advertising the open house. They wanted to be sure they could properly support the number of potential visitors. Even with limited advertising, more than 80 percent of the free tickets were gone days before the month-long open house began. Visitors to the temple included ambassadors, senators, congressmen, and others from fifty-five countries, all ten Canadian provinces and all fifty states of the United States.[1]

More than 53,000 "people from all walks of life and religious backgrounds" attended the forty-minute tour. Brent Belnap, chairman of the temple committee, noted that there was an outward change of demeanor in people as they visited the temple. He saw the "hard-edged New York skepticism" literally melt away, and, by the end of the tour, visitors left with a different tone and attitude.[2]

The ripple effect of the temple's open house in a major news capital like New York reached across the United States and the world. The first sentence of a *USA Today* article stated: "One of the hottest tickets in New York right now is just off Broadway: a tour of a new Mormon temple."[3] The opening statement of a *Los Angeles Times* newspaper article, which was carried by national newspapers from Baltimore to Seattle, stated: "Successfully blending religion with prime real estate, the Mormon Church has completed its first temple in Manhattan."[4] The onslaught of coverage caused the Church's public relations staff to sometimes work fourteen-hour days. Many news outlets covered the open house not just once, but as an ongoing story. Around the world, more than 170 newspapers covered the story, as did major media outlets including CNN, NPR, *World News Tonight*, the *Washington Post*, and *The Wall Street Journal*.[5] President Belnap summed up the coverage: "There has never been so much interest in the Church, as broadly and as favorably, as there has been during the open house. People say the temple is exceeding expectations."[6]

THE HONEYMOON TRAIL

St. George Utah Temple

Completed in 1877, the St. George Utah Temple became the first dedicated temple since the Nauvoo Temple. Members from distant regions, anxious to obtain their temple blessings, began making treks to the temple. For those living south of St. George, a popular route emerged as "The Honeymoon Trail." The Honeymoon Trail had a number of points of origin, but only one destination: the temple in St. George. For some, it started at the Mormon settlements in Arizona such as Snowflake and St. Johns. The trail crossed the Colorado River at Lee's Ferry, went through Pipe Springs, and followed the winter route of the Temple Trail down the Fort Pierce Wash and into St. George.

Among those traveling by buggy or long wagon trains were groups of young couples accompanied by chaperones. With distances so vast and terrain so barren, the trip was truly an extraordinary feat and challenge for young men and women traveling from such remote areas. Anxious for a temple marriage, they often made their journey in the spring and fall while the weather was mild and they weren't needed as much for farm work. En route, their evening encampments included dancing, singing, and storytelling around the campfire. Their honeymoon would be during the two-week wagon ride home. It was arduous, but for those who were young and in love, it was a wonderful start to a life together.

Anna Maria Isaacson, from St. Johns, Arizona, recorded her trip with her groom-to-be, Edwin Marion Whiting, and their friends Sullivan Richardson and Martha Irene (Rene) Curtis:

> When we got to St. George, we rented rooms and Rene and I washed and cleaned all our clothes. That red mud was just the color of the river and you never saw such stuff to get out, especially in white muslin. Finally, on September 27, 1881, we went to the temple in St. George and received our endowments and were married for time and eternity. It was wonderful. I thought we would never make it. On our return trip back to Arizona, Sully and Rene, Edwin and I really enjoyed every minute of it and didn't need any more of a honeymoon.[1]

This marrying tradition, which began in 1878, continued until it was replaced in the 1920s by highways and automobiles. The legacy of "The Honeymoon Trail" is the faith of those young men and women who were willing to travel that rutted, dusty trail in hard-riding wagons to be married in the temple and begin their lives together, raise families, and expand the western frontier.

UNPRECEDENTED RELIGIOUS EVENT

Helsinki Finland Temple

The open house of the Helsinki Finland Temple, 21 September–7 October 2006, gave members living in "the land of the midnight sun" much to celebrate. The response to invitations to attend the three-week event was overwhelming. Although there are only five thousand members of the Church in Finland, an astounding 56,000 people toured the temple, approximately one percent of the nation's entire population. Of this astounding show of support President Gordon B. Hinckley said, "I have participated in the dedication or re-dedication of ninety-four of the one hundred and twenty-four temples. But I have never seen such enthusiasm as I've seen with reference to the Helsinki Temple."[1]

Those who attended the temple quickly spread the word throughout the country that "this is a building you must see." Finnish members, who once viewed their fellow citizens as very secular, were pleasantly surprised with the attendance numbers and positive media reviews. Ville-Matti Karumo, the Church's national director of public affairs and a member of the temple committee, said that they didn't know what to expect. Brother Karumo and the other temple committee members estimated that about 25,000 would likely attend the open house. Within the first few days of tours, it became clear that the estimated attendance numbers would quickly be superseded. Many logistical details pertaining to the open house were swiftly modified to handle the increased number of visitors. Brother Karumo felt that such participation in a religious event was unprecedented in Finland, and that it was a marvelous experience for the Church and the community.[2]

The open house had an immediate and long-lasting effect on the Church in Finland. Full-time missionaries were inundated with requests for lessons, media interviews, and personal deliveries of the Book of Mormon. The members living in Finland witnessed that many people in their country did indeed have interest in religion. The open house of "their" temple will always be a reminder to them that those living in their midst might be more open to gospel truths than had previously been assumed.

Encompassing twelve time zones and straddling two European areas of the Church, the Helsinki Temple has the largest district of any of the Church's temples now functioning. Proceedings of the dedicatory sessions were translated into the languages of the five nations in the temple district: Finnish, Russian, Estonian, Latvian, and Lithuanian.

COME, COME, YE SAINTS
Aba Nigeria Temple

President Gordon B. Hinckley dedicated the Aba Nigeria Temple on 7 August 2005. One week after the temple's dedication, forty-two courageous Saints from Cameroon boarded two elongated minivans—almost minibuses—that were designed to carry eighteen passengers each. Members from the country's two branches were accompanied by senior missionaries Elder and Sister Badger. These Saints embarked on a five-hundred-mile adventure from Yaoundé, Cameroon, to Aba, Nigeria.

The crowded vans traversed twisting roads that included vast unpaved sections. Bouncing along the clay roads, the travelers quickly learned that it was the northern region's rainy season when the dry clay roads turned into slippery mud bogs. The men, most of them wearing their Sunday white shirts and no shoes, cleared the "road" with shovels and pushed the vans from behind. The deep red mire stuck to the sides of the vans and stained much of the passengers' clothing.

After thirty-six hours of arduous travel, the Saints reached the border between Cameroon and Nigeria. Due to discrepancies with the travel documents, border officials forced the two American missionaries to remain at the border, allowing only the Cameroon citizens to continue. As they parted, tears were shed during a brief Church meeting held with all the members. Eighteen hours later, the exhausted travelers finally arrived at the Aba Temple. The travelers were tired yet thrilled to have finally arrived at the temple. All totaled, the originally planned eight-hour ride required just over sixty-four hours of travel time.

After serving in the temple for three days, the group began the trip back home, which was slightly less grueling. Accompanying the vans was a four-wheel-drive vehicle armed with towing straps and winches ready to free the vans from the deep mud. The extra vehicle saved over twelve hours of travel time and also relieved the crowded conditions in the vans. At the Nigerian border, Elder and Sister Badger reunited with the group.

Upon arriving home, everyone agreed it was worth the effort. Endowments had been received, families had been sealed, and baptisms had been performed. Commenting on their member friends, Elder and Sister Badger observed that this temple trip changed many lives. They noted that after that first temple trip, attendance grew at Church meetings. Shortly thereafter, the branch was divided and approval was given for the construction of the Church's first chapel in Cameroon.[1]

BUILDING BRICK BY BRICK
Vernal Utah Temple

On 2 November 1997, the Vernal Utah Temple was dedicated, becoming the first temple to be built out of an existing structure. Built in 1907, the Uintah Stake Tabernacle had served and unified the Vernal community. In the 1970s, the tabernacle was no longer used for Church gatherings, and it fell into disrepair. After years of uncertainty about the building's fate, those appreciating the building's historic value were delighted to receive news from the Church's First Presidency. In a letter read to Church congregations on 13 February 1994, the First Presidency announced, " . . . we have concluded to use the shell of the building, restore its original outside appearance, and create within it a beautiful temple. . . . By so doing the original aspect of the historic structure will be preserved."[1]

With the beginning of construction in the summer of 1995 came a search throughout the area for high-quality period brick to match the brick on the tabernacle walls. This brick would be used to replace damaged bricks and to construct a gateway. Satisfactory brick likely coming from the same clay pit and kiln as those on the original tabernacle was found on only one building. It was a residence owned by a gentleman of a different faith. Once he learned of the Church's interest in his home, he was not sure how he should proceed. After a few sleepless nights, he decided to pray about the situation. He received a

feeling prompting him to contact temple authorities and donate his home to the Church.[2]

More than a thousand volunteers helped dismantle the home. The under-taking required the cleaning of each brick, testing them all for strength, and then carefully placing them on pallets. The endeavor took nearly two months of evenings and Saturdays to complete. Young children to members in their nineties came from throughout the temple district to donate their time and ser-vice. One brother, with his oxygen tank beside him, cleaned bricks while in his wheelchair. When the project was over, about sixteen thousand bricks had been salvaged and prepared to become a permanent part of the beautiful and historic Vernal Utah Temple.[3]

During the demolition of the Uintah Stake Tabernacle's interior, builders needed to get a bulldozer inside the building. They did not know how they were going to get the tractor inside the fragile walls of the aged tabernacle. Conveniently, an archway was discovered in the building's foundation. It was wide enough to allow the tractor to enter the structure—with just inches to spare.[4]

FROM COMMUNISM TO THE TEMPLE

Freiberg Germany Temple

The Freiberg Germany Temple stands on a beautiful site in Freiberg, a city about 120 miles south of Berlin. Cut off from the West from the end of World War II until 1989, the East German Saints remained faithful during their years behind the Iron Curtain, despite their isolation. The history of the Freiberg Germany Temple actually begins with the 1955 dedication of the Bern Switzerland Temple, which had a resounding impact on the Church in East Germany and greatly contributed to the construction of the Freiberg Temple thirty years later.

The Swiss Temple was the first temple to be dedicated in Europe, bringing temple blessings to all European Church members, including those in East Germany, or the German Democratic Republic (GDR). Among those living within the grasp of the communistic regime was President Henry J. Burkhardt. President Burkhardt served in many influential capacities for the Church in East Germany, and he became the first Freiberg Temple president. He served as the Church's main person of contact during most of the GDR's existence. Of this period, President Burkhardt wrote:

> The commandment to the Saints to attend the temple . . .
> remained an important but unfulfilled part of the gospel plan for

everyone in Europe and other parts of the world where no temple existed. Hardly anyone had the expectation of attending a temple during their lifetime, despite their faithfulness to the commandments of God . . . [But] after the temple in Zollikofen [Switzerland] was dedicated in 1955, the wish burned within many Saints to go there. . . . The temple in Zollikofen—so near and yet so far for the members of the GDR—was our [members'] most longed-for goal.[1]

For the first few years following the dedication of the Swiss Temple, many members in the GDR were able to make arrangements to attend the temple. After 1957, the GDR prohibited virtually all members from traveling to the temple. An organized effort to soften the hearts of government officials was made in the early 1970s. President Burkhardt traveled to Berlin and presented three hundred names of members wishing to obtain their temple blessings. The government responded by threatening imprisonment, as he had broken the law by collecting personal information for religious purposes.

In 1978, President Thomas S. Monson was among the Church leaders who formulated a plan for Church members to attend the Swiss Temple. They requested government permission for six couples to attend the temple. Following their return, the names of another six couples would be submitted. The objective was to establish credibility with the government so that eventually hundreds of worthy members would have their turn to obtain their temple blessings. Although this plan was denied, the government countered with an unexpected proposal . . . they suggested that the Church build a temple in the GDR![2]

After the temple's groundbreaking ceremony in 1983, President Monson recorded: "This is a miracle of miracles! . . . It all began when we made a final effort with the government to get permission for our faithful couples to go to the Swiss Temple. The [German] minister in their government then said, 'Why not build a temple in our country?' We took him up on his offer, and the building is now under way."[3]

VISION OF A TEMPLE

Kirtland Temple

The Lord's house in Kirtland provided the setting for remarkable spiritual experiences and for the bestowal of vital priesthood keys. The Lord's house in Kirtland had its genesis in the December 1832 revelations that directed the brethren to "establish a house, even a house of prayer, a house of fasting, a house of faith, a house of learning, a house of glory, a house of order, a house of God" (D&C 88:119). The temple was not to be built after the manner of the world, but according to a plan which the Lord promised to make known (D&C 95:13–14).

In June 1833, the Lord fulfilled his promise to reveal the manner in which the temple should be built. In a vision, Joseph Smith, Sidney Rigdon, and Frederick G. Williams were shown the plans, structure, and design for the temple. Frederick G. Williams later described this experience:

> Carpenter Rolph said, "Doctor [Williams], what do you think of the house"?
>
> [Williams] answered, "It [the blueprint] looks to me like the pattern precisely."
>
> He then related the following: "Joseph [Smith] received the word of the Lord for him to take his two counselors, Williams and

Rigdon, and come before the Lord, and He would show them the plan or model of the house to be built. We went upon our knees, called on the Lord, and the building appeared within viewing distance, I being the first to discover it. Then we all viewed it together. After we had taken a good look at the exterior, the building seemed to come right over us, and the makeup of the Hall seemed to coincide with that I there saw to a minutiae."[1]

While standing inside the temple with Truman O. Angell, one of the supervisors of temple construction, F. G. Williams affirmed again that the completed temple was consistent with the revelation he had seen. Brother Angell recorded in his journal that Williams was unable to see a "difference between it [the vision] and the House as built."[2]

According to Frederick G. Williams's record, the vision he witnessed specifically addressed the Kirtland Temple. However, the design was also applied to the plans for the never-built Independence Missouri Temple. The window layout, floor plan, and interior details for both temples were to be identical.[3]

MORONI STATUE STRANDED ON LOADING DOCK

Taipei Taiwan Temple

The Taipei Taiwan Temple is in a central location in Taiwan's second largest city. The temple's glistening white exterior surrounded by trees and fountains attracts the attention of thousands every day and provides a contrast to the noise and bustle of this busy industrial city.

After the temple's groundbreaking in 1982, construction on the temple proceeded steadily. One of the challenges in building such a significant structure in the tight confines of a city block was the limited space available to store building supplies. Materials used for constructing the temple had to be delivered on a strict time schedule to facilitate an uninterrupted flow in the construction process. In one instance, storage space was provided in an unusual way. When crates containing the baptismal font, twelve large oxen, and the statue of the angel Moroni arrived in the country, customs authorities declined to release them. LaVar Wallgren, who sculpted the statue and the oxen, recalled that the Church authorities did not push the matter because they did not have any place to put them. When the construction officials finally needed them for the temple, they called the custom authorities and said that there were some containers on the dock that had been there for a month or two. The person managing the dock was surprised and, after going through his papers, told them to come and "get these things off the dock!" The whole delay was a blessing in disguise.[1]

LIVES WERE PRESERVED

Logan Utah Temple

During the building of the Logan Utah Temple, several events transpired that were viewed by all who witnessed them as providential escapes from death. In September 1879, Brother Hugh McKay was engaged in masonry work at the top of the southwest corner of the temple. As he took a step backward, his foot slipped through a gap in the boards. His loss of balance caused him to instantly whirl downward to what seemed to be a horrible death. After falling nearly fifty feet, his body, and the fifteen-pound stone he was still holding onto, landed on a pile of loose rock. Two co-laborers administered to the battered man before a doctor arrived. Brother McKay was diagnosed with lacerated fingers and two ribs that were slightly cracked. The temple's historical records state: "How he escaped being dashed to pieces, except through the direct interposition of Providence, is certainly unaccountable." He returned to labor on the temple eleven days later, feeling almost completely recovered.[1]

Another scaffolding accident occurred in August 1883, inside the northwest tower. Three men working on board planks survived a perilous fifty-three-foot fall. One of the workers in the accident was John Knowles, who was administered to by Brother Joshua Salisbury. After he had time to recover, Knowles described his recollection of the events to Salisbury as follows:

I landed so hard that it bounced my spirit right out of my body. I want to tell you that my spirit will never be more free from my body when the Lord calls me home than it was that day. I could see my dead body lying there on the steps. I could hear every word that was said. When my dead body was carried into the office and laid on the couch, Brother John Parry, who had charge of construction, asked one of the men to go get Brother Joshua Salisbury, and [said] "we will administer to him and send him home."

I saw you, Brother Salisbury, fully half a block away, coming up the path from the place where you had been cutting stone for the temple. As you walked, you brushed the stone dust off your sleeves and trousers. You came into the office, poured some water out of the pitcher into the basin, washed your face and hands, then combed your hair and whiskers. Then Brother Parry said, "We will administer to him."

Brother Salisbury, when you said in your prayer, "In the name of Israel's God, we command you to be made whole," my spirit entered my body and I opened my eyes. After it was all over, they put me into the buggy and took me home. I have testified to hundreds of people as to how I was brought back to life through the Priesthood of God.[2]

DOORS OF CONVERSION

Salt Lake Temple

As a member of the Baptist faith, Dorothy Decapot began searching for a Baptist congregation after moving to the small town of Stoughton, Massachusetts. After learning the local community did not have a Baptist church, she began seeking to associate with another group of worshipers. During this period of prayerful searching, she experienced a vivid dream.

In her dream she was walking down a street featuring a variety of attractive church buildings. She noticed a crowd of people lining to enter a beautiful building different from the rest. As she viewed this building, with its many windows and six spires, her whole being began to "radiate with excitement," and she knew she had found the right church. She stood in line and noticed that the large doors she was approaching featured several squares with ornate circles inside them. She turned the door handle only to find that it would not open. She tried again with the same disappointing result. She stepped aside and watched as others entered. Soon, a man dressed in white approached to offer assistance. After she explained her problem, he guided her down the steps, and together they viewed those who were entering. He noted how those who entered were organized by couples and families. He encouraged her to go and return with her family and the doors would then open for her.

Shortly after her dream, two sister missionaries arrived at her door. Dorothy invited the sisters in and began to learn the restored gospel of Jesus Christ. After developing a testimony, Dorothy shared with the sisters details from her dream. The final piece of her conversion came together when the sisters explained that the building she had seen in her dream was the Salt Lake Temple.

Sister Decapot was subsequently baptized, as was her husband several years later. Her dream was literally fulfilled when she arrived at the Salt Lake Temple, this time with her family, and the doors were opened to her.[1]

SHADE FROM THE SUN

Raleigh North Carolina Temple

The weather had a dramatic impact on forming the Raleigh North Carolina Temple's concrete foundation. At the end of May 1999, unseasonably warm weather caused concern for workers preparing to pour the concrete foundation. When the air temperature is too high, concrete can dry too rapidly, causing it to cure improperly and then crack. Although the site was prepared for the pouring, and the cement trucks were coming, the weather was still much too hot.

Temple construction missionary Alaire Johnson, who kept a history of the project, recorded that, out of nowhere, a dark cloud appeared in the clear blue sky and hovered over the area, dropping the temperature about ten degrees. Sister Johnson said that the workers proceeded to pour the concrete, and the cloud remained in position long enough for the concrete to set up perfectly.[1]

MIRACLES FOLLOWED THE COMMITMENT

Johannesburg South Africa Temple

As new converts to the Church in 1970, Alan and Pauline Hogben began longing to be sealed in the temple. At that time, the nearest temple was 5,600 miles away in London, England. After careful financial planning, the couple did not think they could afford the journey until after two years of adhering to a tight budget. Although their temple dreams seemed to be in the distant future, they worked toward getting their temple recommends as soon as possible. To their surprise, however, they were able to be sealed in the London Temple five months after receiving their temple recommends. Brother Hogben described how the miracle took place:

> We were told that the only thing the Lord required of us was to make a commitment, and he would open the doors. So we set out with a very stringent budget that kept our household expenses to a bare minimum. . . . There would come a knock on the door, and someone would bring us a little cake. For months, we would find a food parcel in the back seat of our car after church. Years later, we found that it came from a sister who knew she could never afford to go to the temple, but by helping us she felt she could participate vicariously in our temple experience.[1]

They received further financial aid one evening after sacrament meeting when a member gave them R200 (South African rand), a substantial sum of money in those days. The kind member explained that a man once gave his family a gallon of petrol when they had run out of gas. They had tried to pay him but he said, "No, just give someone else a gallon when they need it." Helping the Hogbens was the way this member felt he could fulfill his obligation to help someone in need. Brother Hogben returned that kindness to others once he returned from the temple. He said, "When we returned from the temple, we gave that R200 to another couple, and they gave it to still another. To this day, we don't know how far that R200 went."[2]

SCRIPTURES AND SUGARCANE

Kona Hawaii Temple

Prior to being selected as the Kona Hawaii Temple architect, John Pharis had completed several projects for the Church throughout the state of Hawaii. He approaches Church projects in a different manner than he does other architectural jobs. He explained, "When I work on a project for the Lord, I always kneel down and pray. As an architect, I always work for my client. And in a sense, when I am working on a House of the Lord or any of His chapels, I am working for the Supreme Client." While fulfilling his duties in building the temple in Kona, Brother Pharis also served as bishop of his ward.

As the temple progressed, and more focus was being given to the temple's interior, John needed to develop designs for the end panels located on the temple's benches. As with other times when key decisions had to be made, he sought divine guidance. He related how the inspiration came:

> I started going through the scriptures to hopefully find an idea. I often counsel my ward members, "If you ever have a problem, just open the scriptures." There are powerful words of communication in the scriptures. God knows we need help and the scriptures are one way He communicates to us. I came home and had a prayer. I randomly opened up the scriptures and my eyes fell right on the immediate

answer to the issue. It was a scripture that explained the parable of the wheat and the tares, and the separation that takes place at the end. I felt it was a wonderful analogy and would be better than just using a hibiscus flower. Since we do not have wheat over here, it would be out of place to put wheat on the end of a bench. What could I do to stylize the story to Hawaii? Then I thought about sugarcane.[1]

Brother Pharis's stylized design depicting sugarcane was given to a gifted wood carver in Laie. The artisan labored diligently to carve and sand to perfection the hard maple panels. Because of inspiration found in the scriptures, the depiction of sugarcane captured in woodwork enhances the temple with beauty and significant meaning.

The Kona Hawaii Temple was dedicated on 23 January 2000 by President Gordon B. Hinckley. On the day of the dedication, hundreds of vibrant red poinsettias adorned the temple grounds. Following the dedicatory services, as President Hinckley exited the temple, members began to reverently sing, "We Thank Thee, O God, for a Prophet." As the prophet waved to them before getting into his car, the multitude, as if on cue, began singing the traditional farewell song "Aloha Oe." An unforgettable spirit of love and gratitude embraced all who were there.[2]

Nearly twenty-six years after its dedication, the São Paulo Brazil Temple was closed for a year and a half for renovation. Before being rededicated, 99,000 visitors toured the temple during its four-week open house. During the four weeks, more than six thousand families requested the missionaries to visit them.[1] On 21 February 2004, prior to the temple's rededication, President Gordon B. Hinckley spoke to members gathered in the historic Pacaembu Stadium. In what was heralded as the largest member meeting held outside the United States, 60,000 members at the stadium and tens of thousands of others located at 184 stake centers gathered to listen to their beloved prophet.[2]

GIVING ALL . . . AND THEN GIVING MORE

São Paulo Brazil Temple

"I have an important announcement," said President Spencer W. Kimball even before the opening hymn and prayer at a Brazil area conference in 1975. "A temple will be built in Brazil; it will be built [here] in São Paulo."[3] The audience gasped, many began to weep, and others let out euphoric cheers. Elder L. Tom Perry called this "the greatest audience reaction I have ever seen."[4]

Since this was the first temple to be built on the South American continent, members from all over South America made significant sacrifices to donate to the temple fund. Elder James E. Faust noted that many followed the Lord's counsel to the Saints in Kirtland: "Come . . . with all your gold, and your silver, and your precious stones . . . and build a house to my name" (D&C 124:26–27).

"They didn't have any money to contribute to the temple fund, or, the money that they managed to save wasn't worth much because of inflation," Elder Faust said. "So they started offering their wedding rings, bracelets, gold medals, diamond rings, graduation rings, and many other personal objects of gold, silver, and precious stones. One member of the Church in Argentina even offered his gold dental cap."[5] When the Saints in South America had reached 60 percent of their quota for donation, a member in São Paulo said: "A lot of [the members] already contributed everything they had. From now on they will have to start giving what they don't have. That is where the real sacrifice will begin."[6]

A TEMPTING PROPOSITION
Nauvoo Temple (1846)

Charles Lambert was converted to the Church while living in England. Desiring to be with the Saints, he made the long journey to Nauvoo. The day after his arrival, he offered his services at the temple site. He was told that there was no money to pay him. Charles replied, "I have not come here to work for pay. I have come to help build that house," pointing to the Nauvoo Temple.

Charles Lambert married during his first year in Nauvoo and assumed the support of his wife's recently orphaned siblings. The Lamberts were forced to get by on very little. During this season of hardship, he often hoped that somehow the money to provide for his family would materialize.

While feeling thus he was passing along the street in Nauvoo one day when he met a well-dressed, genteel stranger who inquired if his name was Charles Lambert. On being told that it was, he said his name was Higgins, and that his home was in Missouri. With an ingratiating smile he said, "I have heard of your skill as a workman, and want you to go to Missouri and work for me. You are not appreciated or properly paid here. If you will quit the Temple and go and work for me, you can name your own price and you will be sure of your pay. You see I have plenty of money with which to pay you." Suiting the

action to the word, he thrust his hand into his pocket, and drew it out full of $10 and $20 gold pieces, which he displayed in a tempting manner, and urged him to accept his offer and not to submit any longer to the unfair treatment accorded him at the Temple.

With a gesture of impatience . . . , Father Lambert thanked the stranger for his offer, but said he couldn't think of accepting it. He said he had no complaint to make of his treatment at the Temple, and the price others would pay for work they wished done would not influence him in the matter, as he intended to continue on at the Temple from principle.

Bidding the stranger "Good-day" he turned to continue his walk along the street, but almost immediately the query arose in his mind as to how the stranger knew his name, and where he got his information from about his skill as a mechanic, and turned to take a final look at the stranger, when lo! He was no-where to be seen. . . . [Charles's] opinion then was . . . that he had been talking with no other than Satan, the prince of tempters, and though he had not yielded to his tempting offer he was vexed with himself for listening to him at all, and especially to his insinuations about the Temple management.[1]

Charles and his wife, Mary Alice, were later sealed in the Nauvoo Temple by John Taylor. When the rest of the Saints left Nauvoo, Charles was called by Brigham Young to remain in Nauvoo and finish the temple. He and his family eventually resided among the Saints in the Salt Lake Valley.

AN INSPIRED SITE SELECTION

St. George Utah Temple

After ten years of struggle to gain a foothold in the desert, St. George's population had reached only twelve hundred. At a council meeting with local leaders on 31 January 1871, Brigham Young officially confirmed the plans to build a temple in the city. Two hilltop locations were proposed. David Henry Cannon Jr., one of the first settlers in St. George, was present when the final site was chosen. He recorded:

> President Young . . . asked them to get into their wagons . . . and with him find a location [site]. To the south they finally stopped.
>
> "But Brother Young," protested the men, "this land is boggy. After a storm . . . no one can drive across the land without horses and wagons sinking way down. There is no place to build a foundation."
>
> "We will make a foundation," said President Young.
>
> Later on, while plowing and scraping where the foundation was to be, my horse's leg broke through the ground into a spring of water. The brethren then wanted to move the foundation line twelve feet to the south, so that the spring of water would be on the outside of the temple.
>
> "Not so," replied President Young. "We will wall it up and leave it here for some future use. But we cannot move the foundation. This spot was dedicated by the Nephites. They could not build it [the temple], but we can and will build it for them."[1]

REMOVING THE CACTUS

Albuquerque New Mexico Temple

In the "land of enchantment," youth of the four New Mexico stakes were among the first to perform labors preparatory to the building of the Albuquerque New Mexico Temple. These hardworking youth prepared the site for the groundbreaking that was to take place on 20 June 1998. The temple site was raw with sagebrush, prickly cactus, cholla plants, and garbage. The army of anxious teens was armed with shovels, rakes, and gloves. After clearing the rubbish and debris, they mowed the weeds and made the site safe for those attending the groundbreaking ceremony.

While working on the temple site, one young man voiced what a great privilege it would be to have a temple nearby and to be worthy to attend it: "We need to clean the cactuses out of our lives before we can enter the temple," he said.

Thanks to these dedicated youth, all those attending the groundbreaking ceremony were able to do so on clean, beautified ground. Among the sixty-five hundred in attendance was a choir of six hundred youth—many of whom had participated in the grounds cleanup.[1]

The Albuquerque New Mexico Temple's beautiful exterior is an indigenous color called desert rose. As the desert sun shines on the temple, the color seems to vary depending on the time of day. The upper portion of the temple is made of gigantic colored concrete panels. Exhaustive measures were taken to ensure that the colored panels matched each other perfectly. To remove any subtle variation in color, crews worked for four months sandblasting the panels and washing them down with acid, using only a sponge.[2]

ALTAR CLOTH SISTERS

Denver Colorado Temple

Tatting is a handmade lace produced by looping and knotting a single strand of heavy thread on a small hand shuttle. All of the altars in the Denver Colorado Temple are gracefully covered with delicately tatted altar cloths. Nineteen uniquely gifted sisters in the Denver Temple district consecrated their time and talents to this labor of love. Some cloths required almost nine hundred hours to complete.

Each of the elegant cloths is unique in appearance and carries with it its own inspirational story of creation. Of her experience, Kathleen P. Bullock said, "I had three children during the four years I worked on my cloth. As you can imagine, the demands on my time were significant. But each time I sat down to work on the cloth, I knew this was something special. I was creating something for the temple that was part of me."[1]

After working on her cloth for a year and a half, Marilyn Gist was within one inch of finishing her masterpiece. Leaving her two-year-old grandson alone for just a moment with her precious cloth proved to be a devastating mistake. "I found him gripping a pair of scissors with both hands just going to town," she said. "He had cut right into the middle and down one side. All I could do was sit down and cry." She coped with the tragedy by putting her tatting supplies away for a few months. Then, with renewed determination, she began tatting a second cloth—a sacrifice of double proportion for the Lord's house.[2]

Some sisters used this opportunity to become self-taught tatting masters, while others worked through the pain of severe arthritis. Just before the temple open house, temple interior designer Lawrence Wyss helped place the sisters' tatted altar cloths on the altars. He recalled his impressions when seeing them within the newly finished temple for the first time: "The tatted cloths were some of the loveliest I've ever seen. As we opened each box we'd draw a breath. Each was so wonderful!"[3]

FROM RAGS TO CARPET

Logan Utah Temple

Just two months before the temple dedication, the temple superintendent of construction asked the Relief Society, Young Ladies Mutual Improvement Association, and the Primary to participate in a carpet-making assignment to offset the cost of having all the carpet made by a carpet manufacturer.

Sisters gathered daily to tear their rags into strips. They would then organize the scraps by color, sew the color-coordinated scraps together, roll them into balls and take them to a weaving machine. The resulting huge rolls of carpet required the assistance of many men to carry and transport them to the temple. This massive undertaking required great skill and long hours. Within just a few weeks of the project's initiation, rolls of carpet began arriving at the temple. The carpets were cut, color-matched, stretched, and hand-sewn together to fit the precise measurements for each room. However, despite the sisters' tireless efforts, they were unable to complete the entire task before the temple dedication. The last of the carpet was installed at 8:00 A.M. on 21 May 1884, just before the first temple ordinance work was to begin for the day.

The manufactured carpet for the temple and the carpet woven by sisters combined to total 3,660 yards, more than two miles of carpeting. Sections of these beautifully crafted floor coverings remained in place for over seventy-five years.[1]

CELESTIAL ROOM GENEROSITY
Baton Rouge Louisiana Temple

As the Baton Rouge Louisiana Temple neared completion, a last-minute decision was made to add three ceiling medallions to the interior. When the medallions arrived, workers noticed that the one intended for the celestial room was damaged. The project manager, Marc Lundin, immediately began searching for a replacement, only to find that the original supplier and all the other dealers he could find did not have the medallion in stock. Even the manufacturer was unable to supply another one.

Finally, with the help of the Internet, Brother Lundin located a dealer in Atlanta, Georgia, who had one left. Brother Lundin gave him the address of the temple in Baton Rouge, and the dealer remarked, "My church is getting ready to dedicate a building in Baton Rouge." Brother Lundin quickly asked, "What church would that be?" When the dealer responded, "The LDS church," Brother Lundin told him that they were both referring to the very same building, and that the medallion would be placed in the celestial room. Brother Lundin then asked what the price of the medallion would be. The Atlanta supplier, J. Doyle Henderson, said he was grateful to have the opportunity to donate the medallion to the temple.[1]

ON THE AMAZON AND OVER THE ANDES

Lima Peru Temple

While temples dot the earth and are being built closer to Church members, some temples can seem to be as distant as ever. Such is the situation for the members living in the jungle-locked city of Iquitos, Peru. Nearly 2,000 miles upriver from the mouth of the Amazon, this city is accessible only by boat or plane. This isolated city is considered one of the most populous cities that cannot be reached by road. For members of the Church, the challenges of traveling to a distant temple are compounded by limited financial opportunities. For members who may not make more than four dollars a day, spending hundreds of dollars for airfare to Lima is an unattainable dream.

After a visit from Lima Temple president J. Marlan Walker, the three stakes of Iquitos began making plans for something they had never attempted—a full-fledged group temple expedition. With air travel out of the question, plans were made for the Saints to travel by boat and bus. To raise money for their river passage, some found additional work, while others sold possessions such as furniture, stoves, and sewing machines. Of their sacrifices, President Walker said, "The people figured those items could be replaced, but they needed to get to the temple."[1]

While travel on the Amazon and Maranon rivers is always adventuresome, the major challenges came while crossing the Andes by bus. Humberto Vilchez, president of the Iquitos Peru Punchana Stake, said that the sixty-five Saints took turns sitting and standing on the bus built to accommodate fifty passengers. President Walker commented that traveling the winding, single-lane, dirt road over the rugged Andes was a petrifying, harrowing experience for the members, and many prayers for a safe passage were uttered. Their six-day journey ended when the buses arrived at the Lima Peru Temple. President Walker recalls watching the weary members step off the bus outside the temple. "The Israelites arriving in the Promised Land could not have had more euphoric looks on their faces than these people from Iquitos arriving at the temple," he said.[2]

For three days these Saints served in the temple, receiving their own endowments, being sealed as families, and doing work for their ancestors. Since the temple does not have patron accommodations, local members opened their homes to provide lodging for the Iquitos members. President Walker observed that despite the long hours and unique circumstances, all served without complaint. The members returned home safely to further build Zion in Iquitos.[3]

RUNNING OUT OF MARBLE

Billings Montana Temple

The baptistry in the Billings Montana Temple is one of the building's many distinctive highlights. The floor pattern and palette of colors are much bolder than that of most temple baptistries. Some building planners considered changing the stone palette to more conservative, lighter colors, but the original plan prevailed, and dark shades of green contrast dramatically with lighter stone.

All of the exquisite marble was imported from Italy and Spain. The temple's interior design team, lead by Bruce Finlinson, had selected specific marble based upon color and grain pattern. Once the purchase orders were placed, temple project superintendent Gale Mair anxiously awaited confirmation from the quarries that the stone had been shipped. Weeks turned into months. Finally, the quarry from Spain reported that they had lost the vein of marble of that particular color and suggested that new colors be selected. The interior designers quickly designed an alternative floor pattern and color scheme. Brother Mair said that during that time of uncertainty he had a spiritual experience indicating that everything was going to be all right and not to worry about it. Just prior to committing to the new floor layout, the Spanish stone quarry called to report that they were able to find the vein again and that they could provide him with all the marble that he needed. The floor was completed as originally planned.[1]

"CTR" MEANS "CHOOSE THE RIGHT"

Edmonton Alberta Temple

An estimated thirty-five hundred people witnessed the groundbreaking for the Edmonton Alberta Temple on 27 February 1999. As the construction commenced, temple construction missionaries Leo C. Udy and Rhea Udy were diligent in their calling to oversee all aspects of construction. Elder Udy reported that achieving the highest quality of work was not difficult because the workers understood that if they didn't do it right the first time they would be back doing it over again, so they carefully read the specifications required and got it right the first time.

Elder Udy remembered a time when the contractors were gathered to discuss an important construction decision. All key personnel gathered to analyze their options on how to solve a specific problem. One option would require less time and money, but the work would be of lesser quality. It was clearly evident that the correct method of construction would take a little longer and cost a little more money. As those gathered continued to debate how to proceed, Elder Udy took off his CTR ring and showed it to the group. He said, "See that? What is on there? It says 'CTR' and that means 'Choose the Right.' That was the end of the discussion and we did it the right way."[1]

NO LIVES WERE LOST

St. George Utah Temple

Ground was broken for the St. George Utah Temple on 9 November 1871. President Brigham Young presided over the historic event and turned over the first shovelful of dirt. A person standing near the prophet recalled that as the prophet turned over the soil, he stated "that there would not be any persons who would lose their lives on any of the works of this temple."[1] Although many persons laboring on the temple were injured, none of them died. So great was their desire to begin building their temple that plows and scrapers began excavating the foundation that very afternoon.

Among those laboring on the temple was Heber Jarvis. He recorded many of his observations and experiences relating to the temple. Of the accidents that transpired during the temple's construction, he wrote:

> One man, by the name of John Burt, fell from the top of the temple. He was plastering with my brother, George Jarvis, who had stepped off a plank. John jumped from the fire wall onto the scaffold about three or four feet below and the plank broke and he went right through, falling to the ground, some 84 feet, and fell on the scattered rock, dirt, etc., which was on the ground. The workmen rushed to him. I was on a horse not far away and came up to him also. He was

conscious and was calling for his mother. In ten days he was walking around the streets of St. George and resumed his work later on, so that the fall did not disable him or prevent him from continuing the work on the temple. . . . Will Thayne fell 35 feet off the wall, alighting across a large malipi rock on his side, but he was not killed; Pete Granger had the large frame from which the huge hammer worked and which weighed many hundreds of pounds, and which was 35 feet high, fall on him; George Lang had a huge rock on his wagon which weighed 8,000 pounds, and was driving a team of mules. His mules ran away with this rock on the wagon; he fell from the wagon, and his ear was torn from his head. Yet none of these men were killed, but continued their labors on the temple.[2]

The temple was completed in six years. The Saints gathered at the temple on New Year's Day of 1877 to dedicate the portions of the building sufficiently completed at that time. President Brigham Young dedicated the entire temple 6 April 1877.

In 1937, the St. George Temple was closed for more than a year due to extensive remodeling. The celestial room chandelier was one of the many items replaced. The new chandelier contained hundreds of delicate crystals. Workers attached a cable and pulley to hoist it into position. As they were inspecting it, it suddenly fell back into its packing box. Fearing the worst, the workers carefully lifted the chandelier back up and began inspecting each crystal for damage. They were grateful to discover that not one piece was broken.[3]

INTERIOR DESIGN CHALLENGES
Lubbock Texas Temple

The construction history of the Lubbock Texas Temple is highlighted by many small miracles.

When some artwork arrived with damaged frames, two men from a local picture-framing business made themselves immediately available to assist in any way. They expertly repaired the broken frames within days, allowing the framed art to be displayed for the open house. Neither man was a member of the Church. Interior designer Greg Hill mentioned that he felt the men were prompted to come and assist.[1]

Another event transpired a few days prior to the open house. A six-foot handcrafted Venetian mirror for the bride's room arrived from Italy broken into many fragments. Greg Hill immediately called the mirror vendor to report the situation. A few days later, a new mirror arrived without any breakage. The new mirror was much better in its overall design and size than the originally ordered mirror. The new mirror seemed to complement the art glass window perfectly and was of better proportions. "The Lord knew what He wanted, even if we didn't," said Hill.[2]

On the morning the furnishings were being unpacked and brought into the temple, it was discovered that a vase shipped from Salt Lake City was broken in several pieces. This imported crystal Italian vase—adorned with etched

grapevines—had been ordered months earlier and was available only by special order. As efforts were made to order a replacement, the Salt Lake City company reported that an individual in Salt Lake City had recently ordered exactly the same vase, but had returned it after determining that it was too large for his use. The company shipped the new vase to Lubbock and it arrived in perfect condition. This vase was placed prominently on a pedestal in the entrance to the temple and is filled with white calla lilies. An identical vase is also found at the entrance to the Salt Lake Temple.[3]

As the elegant furnishings were brought into the celestial room, another problem was discovered. One of the armchairs had a five-inch-long slit running down the middle of the fabric. The delicate fabric had been cut by a box cutter when it was unpacked. To remedy the situation, Greg Hill said he felt prompted to call a specific local upholstery firm. The company explained their policy was to work only on furniture for which they supplied the fabric, and they were busy for the next two months. "Once again the Lord heard our prayers and answered them," said Hill. A woman from the company called back and said they would be happy to help. The chair was repaired and delivered to the temple two days later.[4]

THE RIGHT STONE AT THE RIGHT PRICE

Newport Beach California Temple

From announcement to dedication, many challenges impeded the progress of the Newport Beach California Temple. One of these obstacles included the selection of the temple's surface stone. Initially, the Church proposed that the temple be clad with the same dazzling white granite that adorns the Redlands California Temple. However, the stone color had to be approved by the city, several local citizens' groups, and the seller of the property (the Irvine Company). Perhaps as a reaction to the neighborhood opposition to a very light stone, the Irvine Company in 2001 rejected four separate stone samples submitted by the Church. A year later, an earth-toned granite named "Salisbury Pink" was approved for the temple.

After being quarried from an island off the shore of North Carolina in 2003, some Salisbury granite was sent by the Church to China for hand carving. The Church was not able to acquire more because a large quantity of the existing Salisbury granite was commissioned for an elaborate palace in the Middle East and had been sent to Italy. Progress on the palace eventually came to a halt, leaving a large surplus of granite in Italy, which the Church was able to acquire at a fraction of the original price. In the end, the series of arduous delays that occurred while selecting the stone became an apparent blessing. The timing of the stone approval and the resulting stone selection allowed the right stone to be used on the temple at a substantial savings.[1]

Newport Beach Temple architect Lloyd Platt explained that he is ultimately responsible to make sure a temple is completed to the strictest quality specifications. According to Brother Platt, "the finished product must be perfection. Only the highest quality of woodwork, plaster, paint and so on, will be acceptable. Every tiny nick will be marked on and fixed before the Church accepts the building."[2]

Assisting with the enforcement of these high standards on the temple was project superintendent Vernon Forbush. He explained how interior walls may appear to be perfectly straight and smooth in daylight; however, the real test is at night in perfect darkness. In the dark, Brother Forbush inspected the walls by shining a flashlight down them, which exposed any imperfections. On many occasions workers had to "refloat," or apply additional wall compound, to eliminate any variation.[3]

A SPECIAL DEDICATORY SESSION

Lima Peru Temple

In January 1986, nearly five years after it was announced, the Lima Peru Temple was dedicated. President Gordon B. Hinckley presided over the dedicatory sessions. The dedicatory prayer he offered included these words: "Surely father Lehi has wept with sorrow over his posterity. Surely he weeps today with gladness." During the service he also said, "The day has arrived. Lehi, Sariah, Nephi, and others in that other sphere are rejoicing. This is the day of salvation for generations."[1]

Indeed, this long-awaited day was a day of rejoicing. Members from many South American nations made a valiant effort to participate in the day's sacred and historic events. But some, despite their best efforts, were not able to arrive at the temple in time for the scheduled dedicatory services. A group of Bolivian Saints were en route to the dedication when their bus began having a series of mechanical breakdowns. Worried that they would miss their dedicatory session, they called the temple several times to tell them they were on their way. When President Gordon B. Hinckley learned of their plight and realized they would miss the last session, he replied, "The next time they call, let them know that whenever they arrive there will be a session for them, even if it's 2:00 in the morning."[2]

CONVERTED WHILE BUILDING A TEMPLE

Raleigh North Carolina Temple

Gary Stansbury, an expert in building mega-projects, had planned on building a $65 million shopping complex. Not a member of the Church, he was disappointed when the shopping complex project was delayed and he was asked to be the project superintendent for the more modest Raleigh North Carolina Temple. When the temple was delayed over building permits, Gary began to consider other offers.

As soon as the temple construction began, Gary said, "I didn't want to leave." It did not take long for Gary to develop a respect and friendship with temple construction missionaries Gaylen and Alaire Johnson. The temple served as a natural visual aid for the Johnsons to teach Gary about the restored gospel while they worked with him at the temple site.

Gary explained that while studying the Book of Mormon he gained a testimony of "building only that which is worth building," and he felt that that was exactly what he was doing.[1] Elder Johnson baptized Gary in September 1999. At his confirmation, Bishop Bruce Nay of the Apex Ward commented, "Most people come to the temple by way of the gospel; Gary came to the gospel by way of the temple."[2]

Brother Stansbury reflected: "Looking back at the series of events that brought me here to North Carolina, I don't much believe in coincidence. There were just too many things that fell into place."[3]

The Salt Lake Temple has 253,000 square feet. The Raleigh North Carolina Temple has 10,700 square feet—about 1/25th the size of the Salt Lake Temple.

Upon completion, the Raleigh North Carolina Temple set a record for the fastest completion of a temple. The temple required about two hundred days to build, forty days less than the average for similar smaller temples.

Architects of the São Paulo Brazil Temple went to great lengths to make the temple sturdy and capable of withstanding a major earthquake with minimal damage. Its foundation is said to be strong enough to sustain thirteen additional stories. Some scoffed at the Church's precautionary measures. At the time, Brazil was considered to be an earthquake-free country, but during construction a small earthquake shook downtown São Paulo. The following day newspapers were filled with articles by local scientists reporting that more earthquakes of greater magnitude were likely to occur in the future.[1]

AN AMAZON EXODUS

São Paulo Brazil Temple

The São Paulo Brazil Temple was the first temple to be built on the continent of South America. Even with a temple in South America, most Saints in the temple district had to travel long distances to the temple and make tremendous financial sacrifices. One memorable journey began on an early morning in November 1992, as a small passenger boat cast off from the pier at the Port of Manaus, a Brazilian city deep in the heart of the Amazon jungle. One hundred and two anxious Latter-day Saints were on board as the boat traveled down a network of rivers, finally reaching the powerful Amazon. Because these Saints' limited resources made air travel impossible, they traveled continuously for six days and nights by boat and bus to reach the temple. While aboard, the passengers celebrated the eighth birthday of one of the children. The boat stopped at a port, and after checking to be sure the water was free of alligators and piranhas, the father baptized his daughter. On the fourth day, the Saints left the more commodious boat and endured two wearying days of bus travel beset by mechanical breakdowns and rough roads.

Arriving at the temple, they were immediately involved in the work. They spent four days basking in the joy of temple service, many for the first time. At the end of another six days and nights of travel, these stalwart Saints arrived safely back in Manaus, forever changed by their journey.[2]

LAND PRESERVED FOR A TEMPLE

Detroit Michigan Temple

In 1956 the Church bought nearly eight acres of land for construction of the greater Detroit area's first stake center. The stake center takes up only part of this land, and many thought that the Church should sell the remaining acreage. George Romney, the first stake president in Michigan and, at one time, the governor of the state, felt strongly that the land should not be sold. Decades later, stake president Thomas C. Bithell, who was in charge of finding a site for the temple, at first dismissed the lot as too small for the temple. However, after reviewing several other properties, President Bithell looked again at the lot from his office window in the Bloomfield stake center. It was measured, "and I was very surprised at the size of this lot," he said. "The more I looked and contemplated, the more this seemed to be the right location."[1]

Over the years, the property where the temple now stands has been landscaped with grass and a variety of trees. Members have always kept the grounds free of weeds and litter. Many remember holding various outdoor activities on the property. On 10 October 1998, at the temple's groundbreaking ceremony, President Bithell observed, "To the best of my knowledge, nothing has ever been built on this property. It is sacred ground, preserved for this very purpose."[2]

The history of the Church in the Detroit area began with Lucy Mack Smith, mother of the Prophet Joseph Smith. In 1831, Lucy traveled to Michigan to visit the family of her brother Colonel Stephen Mack, founder of Pontiac, Michigan. Stephen Mack, the proprietor of a large mercantile establishment in Detroit, built a turnpike from Detroit to his farm in Pontiac at his own expense. That same road now runs in front of the temple and is known today as Woodward Avenue. The Prophet Joseph himself may have stood on the grounds of the temple site during his 1834 visit to Detroit, when he likely traveled this road to his uncle's home.[3]

A HOME FOR THE TEMPLE PRESIDENT

Lubbock Texas Temple

The Lubbock Texas Temple is built on property acquired in the late 1980s for the building of the Lubbock Texas Stake Center. The purchased parcel was much larger than was needed for the stake center and, following the building's dedication in 1989, efforts were made to sell off the excess property. The sale of the property never transpired because the acreage lacked street access. This failed transaction developed into a blessing when, in the spring of 2000, the ground was deemed to be the prime location for a temple.

In addition to securing a temple site location, a nearby house needed to be purchased as the residence of the temple president. The most desirable home that was contiguous with the temple property was not for sale. A meeting was arranged with the owners to prepare them for the impending construction activities and to again inquire if the home could be purchased. The offer was declined. The next morning the owners called to ask if the Church would still consider buying their home. This home was purchased, refurbished, and furnished as the temple president's residence.[1]

THE MIRACLE OF THE FISHES AND LOAVES OF BREAD

Nauvoo Illinois Temple (2002)

The 127 historically designed windows of the Nauvoo Illinois Temple are one of the temple's most distinctive features. The windows were crafted in Nauvoo by Charles Allen and his coworkers at the Allyn Historic Sash Co. To accomplish this task, the company tripled the work space, hired additional crew, and allowed longer work days. Many of the workers acknowledge that divine blessings made it possible for problems to be resolved and deadlines to be met.

One of these blessings occurred during the process of waterproofing the wood. The raw wood had to be dipped twice in water repellent prior to receiving coats of primer and paint. One day, after treating about twenty sashes, workers John Howell and Dan Hahl were concerned about running out of the repellent. Charles Allen recorded in his journal:

> John and Dan came in and said they had witnessed the "miracle of the fishes and loaves of bread"! They had been putting a cup of repellent in their container after dipping three or four sash[es] to keep it at the level needed. When that ran out, they kept on dipping, without replacing any repellent and finished all forty-seven sash[es]. They then poured out what was left in the dipping container and filled a full gallon and a few cups more. It was a miracle to behold. Our work truly is an inspired process.[1]

The elliptical window on the east end of the Nauvoo Temple celestial room is the largest window in the temple. It includes 234 pieces of glass. The window frame alone is 22½ feet wide, 8½ feet tall, and weighs approximately 1,000 pounds. The glass within the windows is from a factory in Saint Just, France. About 6,000 square feet of mouth-blown cylinder glass, created using Old World techniques, adorn the windows of the temple.[2]

THE LORD LOANED HIM TO US

St. George Utah Temple

In 1896, George and Avis Rogers desired to travel to the St. George Utah Temple with their eight-month-old boy to be sealed as a family. As they prepared for the lengthy trip, their baby boy became terribly sick with pneumonia and was "given up by the doctor." Avis prayed for the Lord to spare her son long enough to allow them to be sealed as a family. George and two other priesthood brethren administered to him and "in just a short time he began to get better," said Avis. "It was a testimony of the power of the priesthood and faith to us; and as soon as the opportunity came for us to go to St. George . . . we did so."

Along the way, the little family was terrorized by Indians with painted faces. As Avis stared at them in horror, her husband George kneeled in prayer, petitioning Heavenly Father to protect his family from the Indians. The braves continued whooping as they disappeared into the night. Avis said, "We knew that the Lord had answered our prayers as he had done so many times before."

After their seven-week journey to and from St. George, the young family arrived back home. After being home for a few weeks, Avis recorded the following: "Our baby took sick again, just like the first time, and once again it was up to our Heavenly Father. He passed away December 13, 1897. We always knew the Lord had loaned him to us for a while longer so we could have the privilege of taking him to the temple . . . and we were always grateful for this."[1]

A BELL WITH A LEGACY

Nauvoo Temple (1846)

The graceful tower of the Nauvoo Temple featured a 1,500-pound bell paid for by British Saints. The bell was cast in bronze in England and brought by Wilford Woodruff to Nauvoo. When mobs forced the Saints to evacuate the city, the bell was left behind and placed in a local Protestant church. It was recovered by the Lamoreaux family before they headed west.

> One stormy night the men gathered in secret and without horses pulled the wagon to the Church and lowered the Bell, pushed and pulled the wagon by hand to the edge of the Mississippi River and carefully concealed it in the water. Andrew Lamoreaux and his brother, David, were chosen to bring the Bell to Utah with their families, concealing the Bell in their wagon with their provisions.[1]

On the journey west, the bell was used to signal various activities. Once in Salt Lake City, and after having been moved several times, it was finally placed in 1942 into its permanent home in the bell tower on Temple Square, which fulfilled a prophecy by Brigham Young: "Right west of the temple we shall build a tower and put a bell on it. . . . This plan was shown to me in a vision when I first came onto the ground."[2]

In 1961 President David O. McKay, presiding at a ceremony at KSL-TV, said: "In its own way, the Nauvoo bell is a symbol of religious freedom in our land. . . . When we hear, henceforth, the sound of the Nauvoo bell, let it remind us anew that our nation and our community owes its existence to our trust in God."[3]

Today the bell rings at the beginning of each hour. The ring of the bell has been featured for years on KSL radio to mark the "top of the hour." The ringing of the Nauvoo bell can be controlled by a panel on the Mormon Tabernacle organ. The bell is also rung on special occasions, such as the memorial services held on 14 September 2001 for those who died in the terrorist attacks on the United States of America.

The new Nauvoo Illinois Temple features a 1,000-pound, bronze-alloy replica of the original bell. The new bell features the engravings for two years, 2001 (the year of its casting) and 2002 (the year of the temple's completion). It is pitched to chime near an F sharp on the musical scale. On 21 September 2001, spectators cheered as a statue of the angel Moroni was set into place and the bell in the temple's domed tower chimed seven times.[4]

FINDING PROPERTY IN HONG KONG

Hong Kong China Temple

When President Hinckley traveled to Hong Kong in 1992 to consider several potential temple sites, he felt unsatisfied with all of them. "We looked at one after another after another. I became very discouraged," he later said. "The sites were so tiny in some respects and the cost of real estate is so high—many millions of dollars for a little piece of ground."[1]

One night, he retired with no clear understanding of how he should proceed on his assignment to find a location for the temple, but in the middle of the night he awoke with an impression. He recorded: "Something very interesting came into my mind. I did not hear a voice with my natural ears. But into my mind there came the voice of the Spirit. It said, 'Why are you worried about this? You have a wonderful piece of property where the mission home and small chapel stand. They are in the very heart of Kowloon, in the location with the best transportation. . . . Build a building of [several] stories. It can include a chapel and classrooms on the first two floors and a temple on the top two or three floors.' . . . I relaxed and went back to sleep."[2]

"To me it was inspiration," President Hinckley said. "I drew [the temple] out, and I still have the little drawing that I made . . . in my journal. [This drawing] is essentially the plan which we had for this temple."[3]

MY ANGEL MOTHER

Salt Lake Temple

Moroni has been identified as the angel mentioned in Revelation 14:6 as "having the everlasting gospel to preach unto them that dwell on the earth, and to every nation, and kindred, and tongue, and people." The statue of the angel Moroni holding a trumpet and heralding the gospel to the world is one of the most well-known iconic symbols of the Church. The first temple to feature an angel Moroni statue was the Salt Lake Temple. The statue was placed on the temple's 210-foot-high eastern central spire during a capstone ceremony on 6 April 1892, one year to the day before the temple was dedicated.

Church President Wilford Woodruff extended the commission of designing the first angel Moroni statue to artist Cyrus E. Dallin. The Utah-born, non-LDS Dallin is considered one of America's most talented and prolific sculptors. Dallin initially declined the commission, stating that he did not believe in angels and felt someone with a "greater spiritual capacity" should be given the opportunity. However, his strongly religious mother encouraged him to reconsider. When he explained to her that he did not believe in angels, she reminded him, "Every time you return home and take me in your arms you call me your 'angel mother.'"[1] Dallin accepted the commission and proceeded to study the scriptures and other Church doctrine to gain better insight into Moroni's character.

When the statue was positioned into place atop the temple, both Cyrus Dallin and President Wilford Woodruff were present. It is reported that President Woodruff turned to Dallin and asked, "Now, Mr. Dallin, do you believe in angels?"

His response was, "Yes, my mother is an angel."[2]

Reflecting on the vast numbers of masterpiece sculptures he had created, Dallin said, "I considered that my 'Angel Moroni' brought me nearer to God than anything I ever did. It seemed to me that I came to know what it means to commune with angels from heaven. . . . We can only create in life what we are and what we think."[3]

Cyrus Dallin's angel Moroni statue established the general pattern for further statues of angel Moroni on the spires of subsequent temples. This statue depicts a dignified neoclassical angel in robe and cap, standing upright with a trumpet firmly in hand. The original three-foot plaster model was completed in October 1891 and sent to Salem, Ohio, where it was hammered into a twelve-foot copper statue and then covered with delicate 22-karat gold leaf.[4]

ANCESTORS DRESSED IN WHITE

Manti Utah Temple

Anthon Henrik Lund was ordained a member of the Quorum of the Twelve Apostles in 1889. Elder Lund also served as the Manti Temple president from 1891 to 1893. During his service as the temple president, he recorded the following miraculous experience:

I remember one day in the temple at Manti, a brother from Mount Pleasant rode down to the temple to take part in the work, and as he passed the cemetery in Ephraim, he looked ahead (it was early in the morning), and there was a large multitude all dressed in white, and he wondered how that could be. Why should there be so many up here; it was too early for a funeral, he thought; but he drove up and several of them stepped out in front of him and they talked to him. They said, "Are you going to the temple?"

"Yes."

"Well, these that you see here are your relatives and they want you to do work for them."

"Yes," he said, "but I am going down today to finish my work. I have no more names and I do not know the names of those who you say are related to me."

"But when you go down to the temple today you will find there are records that give our names."

He was surprised. He looked until they all disappeared, and drove on.

As he came into the temple, Recorder Farnsworth came up to him and said, "I have just received records from England and they all belong to you." And there were hundreds of names that had just arrived, and what was told him by these persons that he saw was fulfilled. You can imagine what joy came to his heart, and what a testimony it was to him that the Lord wants this work done."[1]

THE "MCKAY OAK" LEGACY

London England Temple

After the property for the London England Temple was purchased in 1952, President David O. McKay and temple architect Edward O. Anderson toured the beautiful grounds. One of the grandest tree specimens growing on the old Elizabethan farm was an enormous oak tree with a circumference of twenty-one feet. The tree was estimated to have existed at the time of Columbus's discovery of the Americas. After viewing the tree, President McKay gave strict instructions that the mighty oak was not to be uprooted.[1]

Local members thought of their prophet with affection when viewing the oak and subsequently attached a plaque to it identifying the tree as "The David O. McKay Oak."[2] After decades of enhancing the temple's pastoral setting, the tree finally died.

Several years prior to the tree's demise, Church landscaping supervisor Irvin T. Nelson brought nearly two hundred of the ancient tree's acorns to Salt Lake City. He planted and nurtured the acorns in pots located on Temple Square. Of the many acorns planted, two of the them matured into small trees. When the trees were four years old, Brother Nelson showed them to President McKay, who received them with a big smile. Brother Nelson affectionately named each of the trees "President David O. McKay Oak Jr."[3]

In 1972, Peter Lassig succeeded Irvin Nelson as Temple Square landscaping supervisor. Brother Lassig planted one of the "McKay Oak Jr." trees behind the Aaronic Priesthood monument. There in the shadows of the Salt Lake Temple, it grew well and matured into an attractive and large tree. In 2002, construction work on Temple Square required that the oak tree be removed. Thankfully, six months prior to construction, Brother Lassig had the foresight to harvest hundreds of acorns from the tree and send them to the London Temple to be planted on the grounds as the "grandchildren" of the original "David O. McKay Oak."[4]

Great credit is due to the faithful and skillful service of Brothers Irvin Nelson and Peter Lassig. Due to their efforts, there are now many oak trees on the London Temple grounds growing with beauty and a meaningful legacy.

A SITE OVERLOOKING THE CITY

Guayaquil Ecuador Temple

The long ministry of Gordon B. Hinckley was consistently focused on the building of temples. As President of the Church, he increased his personal involvement with every phase of temple work and temple building. Among the responsibilities he treated with the highest priority was the selection of locations for the House of the Lord. Whenever possible, he selected the exact site himself. "President Hinckley has tromped around countless hills looking for temple sites," said Elder Neal A. Maxwell. "It is not his way to sit back and have the temple committee say, 'We think a temple is needed here and we have found a location.' He wants to walk to the top of the hill himself and feel what there is to be felt there. It is almost as though he has always felt a responsibility to President McKay for temples and temple work."[1] One of the many examples of President Hinckley's personal involvement in a temple site selection occurred in Guayaquil, Ecuador. After an intense search, Church leaders in the area real estate department prepared six locations for President Hinckley's review. President Hinckley examined the locations one by one and was not interested in any of them. He requested to return to the first location and, while reviewing the site for the second time, he asked what lay beyond a group of trees on the adjacent property. While exploring the new area by car they found an unpaved road. Brother Philippe Kradolfer, who was serving as director of temporal affairs for the South America North Area, remembers that when the prophet saw this road, he said, "This is precisely where we are going." Brother Kradolfer continued, "The little road led to a gorgeous piece of property that oversees the whole of Guayaquil. None of us said a word as President Hinckley got out of the car and walked to the edge of the property. As he stood alone looking down upon the city, tears filled my eyes because I knew that a prophet had found the site for the temple."[2]

FINDING GREAT JOY IN GIVING

Newport Beach California Temple

After the Newport Beach California Temple was announced in the spring of 2001, members throughout the temple district expressed the desire to donate funds to the building of the temple. After receiving approval from Church headquarters, stakes within the temple district invited members to contribute to the temple building fund. Newport Beach stake president Weatherford T. Clayton explained that their hope was to relieve the Church of the responsibility of finding the funds to construct the Newport Beach temple so that that money could be used to build temples in less affluent areas. Church members were honored and eager to accept the responsibility to fund the temple. Many faith-promoting experiences were had by those who sacrificed to build this temple. With great joy, many who had almost nothing found ways that they could contribute. President Clayton shared his thoughts further: "It was a great experience as a stake president to discuss this with families. . . . We as members cannot build temples like they did in the old days but at least we can help pay for them."[1] This period of giving to the temple often became the theme of sacrament meeting talks and Sunday School lessons. It brought an additional sense of unity among the Saints who realized this as a once-in-a-lifetime opportunity. The goal date to have the temple paid for was March 2004. The faithful Saints of the temple district reached this goal well in advance of the date with an additional surplus of funds.

Before the Newport Beach Temple was built, archaeologists excavated the entire site where the temple now stands. Thousands of remnant artifacts were discovered from a variety of different period civilizations. A ceremonial crystal was found that was dated to the year 600 BC. Nearby archaeological sites provided evidence of ancient wars, burial grounds, and buildings. The temple site, however, had artifacts supporting the hypothesis that the site was used for resting, eating, ceremonies, and other peaceful purposes.[2]

ONLY THE WHITEST MARBLE

Louisville Kentucky Temple

The Louisville Kentucky Temple rests on a forested hill saturated with dense green. This deep green provides an impressive backdrop to the temple's stunning white surface. Although the Danby Vermont marble used on the temple is considered white, the marble actually has a wide range of gray shades and dark veins. To ensure that only the whitest of marble was placed on the temple, the slabs of marble had to be sorted. The tedious process of hand selecting the purest marble was accomplished by temple construction missionary Elder Marvin Prestridge.

The process began by first establishing parameters of what was acceptable. Elder Prestridge personally examined every piece of marble. Of the first seven pallets of marble delivered, over 40 percent of the incoming stone was rejected. He removed every nine-pound piece of marble from the crate and then laid the pieces in an area of about forty square feet. He sorted all of the pieces by color and pattern. He wanted to make sure that every piece of marble in the temple had a white background. His sorting technique attracted a lot of attention. Many inquired why he was going to such great effort. He responded simply by saying, "The temple needs to be as white as possible."

In total, the temple and the site's retaining walls required 22,000 square feet of marble. Elder Prestridge estimates he handled and examined just under two hundred thousand pounds of marble.[1]

DETERMINED TO SERVE IN THE TEMPLE

Los Angeles California Temple

Jan Dickson had a difficult time attending the Los Angeles California Temple due to her advanced case of fibromyalgia, which prevented her from sitting for long periods of time. On one occasion while serving in the temple, the pain left her in agony for days afterward. She prayed for a way to open up that would allow her to attend the temple without suffering. She said, "I prayed for days, weeks, months."

One day Sister Dickson received a phone call from a ward member, Rosa Rice, who felt she was prompted to call and check on her. Sister Dickson shared her desire to attend the temple and described her medical condition that hindered her from her goal. As they considered many options, they concluded that the only way Sister Dickson could attend the temple was if she were lying down.

Sister Rice called the Los Angeles Temple, explained the unique situation, and received permission for Sister Dickson to be able to lie down during the session. The temple presidency said they would welcome her to attend. When she heard the news, Sister Dickson exclaimed, "I was dumbfounded. I almost didn't believe it!"

On 12 November 1992, Sister Dickson attended the temple for the first time in six years. The temple provided a gurney, which eased her pain. Of the special day she described, "As I entered the temple . . . I had trouble controlling the tears in my eyes. I was so grateful." With this new option provided her, she was able to start again attending the temple once a month.[1]

A WORTHY TRADE SPECIALIST

Frankfurt Germany Temple

Tobias Rosendahl and his family actively served in their Muenster Branch near Dortmund Germany. His employment was installing specialty awnings and outdoor blinds. During a particularly slow work period, he felt a strong desire to serve in the temple near Frankfurt. He and his mother-in-law, Donna Hessling, gathered family names and made the nearly three-hour autobahn journey together.

To their great surprise, there was not one car in the parking lot. A security person soon greeted them and explained the temple was closed for two weeks for maintenance. Although the temple closure had been announced throughout the temple district, the news had not reached Brother Rosendahl.

As he and Sister Hessling sat in their car discussing what they should do, a delivery truck arrived. The truck driver was a member of the temple's maintenance crew. The worker invited the two temple visitors into the temple, where others suggested that they could help clean. With enthusiasm they thought, "We came all the way from Muenster to work in the temple. To help clean is also temple work." As they cleaned, Brother Rosendahl was told that among the many items needing repair were the newly installed temple blinds. He later learned that he was the only qualified German installer with a temple recommend who could do the job. During the next few weeks he visited the temple several times to fix and install motors for the new blinds. He was the answer to many prayers.[1]

LIGHTNING STRIKES

St. George Utah Temple

Brigham Young followed the progress of the St. George Utah Temple with great satisfaction. There was one thing he did not like about the temple design, however. He felt the tower on the temple was "short and squatty," and he boldly encouraged the members to rebuild it higher.[1] The people, worn out after their nonstop efforts to build the temple, resisted. Five months after the temple was dedicated, President Young died in Salt Lake City at age seventy-six. Several weeks later, on the night of 16 October 1878, a severe storm hit St. George, and at 3 A.M. the tower was struck by lightning. A letter to President Wilford Woodruff describing the damage states: "We find in repairing the roof that the hand of the Lord, and nothing else, must have saved the building from being burnt at the time the tower was struck by lightning."[2]

The tower was promptly rebuilt—this time with a taller, more majestic tower. The unanimous feeling of the St. George Saints was that President Young finally had his way. The story told in the *Color Country Spectrum* dated 13 April 1977, observed, "He [Brigham Young] was not able to convince those people to put on a tall tower rather than a short dome . . . at least not in this life."[3]

In 1994, the original wooden tower of the St. George Temple was replaced with an exact replica made out of fiberglass. Rather than throw the "tower wood" away, the temple presidency devised an ingenious way to use the historic wood. The wood was carefully crafted into picture frames displaying the pencil drawing of the St. George Utah Temple by artist Chad S. Hawkins. The artist signed the prints and donated them to this worthy project. All of the frames included an original square pioneer nail positioned on the front. Each precious frame was presented to temple workers serving at that time.[4]

NOTES

EXPEDITION OF FAITH

1. Thane Hales and Joan M. Hales (West Africa public affairs missionaries), interview by author, audio recording, 23 May 2007.

2. "U.S. Ambassador Tours Temple Site, *Church News*, 16 August 2004, 15.

TIMELESS AND SACRED GROUND

1. Ingvar Olsson (Stockholm temple recorder), privately published document, 30 October 2004.

THE HOTTEST TICKET ON BROADWAY

1. Shaun D. Stahle, "Manhattan Temple Ready for Dedication June 13," *Church News*, 12 June 2004.

2. Carrie A. Moore, "N.Y. Temple to Get Spire," *Deseret News*, 10 June 2004.

3. Cathy Lynn Grossman, "Mormons Open Temple Doors to Share Beliefs," *USA Today*, 26 April 2004.

4. John J. Goldman, "Mormons Move into Manhattan," *Los Angeles Times*, 9 May 2004.

5. Scot and Maurine Proctor, "The Manhattan Temple Dedication—A Photographic Essay," *Meridian Magazine*, June 2004, www.ldsmag.com.

6. Shaun D. Stahle, "World Looks at New York Temple," *Church News*, 15 May 2004.

THE HONEYMOON TRAIL

1. Anna Maria Isaacson in Norma Baldwin Ricketts, *Arizona's Honeymoon Trail: Mormon Wagon Roads* (Mesa, AZ: Cox Printing, 2001), 23.

UNPRECEDENTED RELIGIOUS EVENT

1. "Helsinki Finland Temple Impact," The World Report of The Church of Jesus Christ of Latter-day Saints, April 2007, http:www.lds.org/ldsnewsroom/eng/the-news-report/april-2007

2. Ville-Matti Karumo, interview by author, audio recording, 8 October 2006.

NOTES

COME, COME, YE SAINTS

1. Franklin Alonzo Badger and Lynda Badger (Yaoundé Cameroon senior missionaries), interview by author, audio recording, 29 May 2007.

BUILDING BRICK BY BRICK

1. Kathleen M. Irving and John D. Barton, *From Tabernacle to Temple: The Story of the Vernal Utah Temple* (Vernal, UT: S. T. Tabernacle Enterprises, 1998), 31.

2. Matthew R. Foley (project supervisor for dismantling project), "The Meagher or Reader Home," unpublished document, copy in possession of author, used by permission.

3. Ibid.

4. Irving and Barton, *Tabernacle to Temple*, 51.

FROM COMMUNISM TO THE TEMPLE

1. Henry J. Burkhardt, "Wie es zum Bau des Freiberger Tempels kam," 1983, trans. Raymond M. Kuehne, in Raymond M. Kuehne, "The Freiberg Temple: An Unexpected Legacy of a Communist State and a Faithful People," unpublished, 2.

2. Kuehne, "Freiberg Temple," 2–9.

3. Thomas S. Monson, *Faith Rewarded: A Personal Account of Prophetic Promises to the East German Saints* (Salt Lake City: Deseret Book, 1996), 88.

VISION OF A TEMPLE

1. Frederick G. Williams quoted in Truman O. Angell's "Journal," in Elwin C. Robison, *The First Mormon Temple—Design, Construction, and Historic Context of the Kirtland Temple* (Provo, UT: Brigham Young University Press, 1997), 8.

2. Ibid., 24.

3. Robison, *First Mormon Temple*, 9.

MORONI STATUE STRANDED ON LOADING DOCK

1. LaVar Wallgren, interview by author, audio recording, 5 January 2000.

NOTES

LIVES WERE PRESERVED

1. Nolan P. Olsen, *Logan Temple: The First 100 Years* (Logan, UT: Keith W. Watkins and Sons Inc., 1978), 74.

2. Ibid., 75–76.

DOORS OF CONVERSION

1. Dorothy Decapot, correspondence with author, dated 20 July 2006.

SHADE FROM THE SUN

1. Alaire Johnson, "Temple Project History," unpublished manuscript, 5, copy in author's possession.

MIRACLES FOLLOWED THE COMMITMENT

1. R. Val Johnson, "South Africa: Land of Good Hope," *Ensign*, February 1993.

2. Ibid.

SCRIPTURES AND SUGARCANE

1. John Pharis (architect of the Kona Hawaii Temple), interview by author, audio recording, 21 January 2000.

2. As recorded in author's journal.

GIVING ALL . . . AND THEN GIVING MORE

1. "99,000 Visit São Paulo Temple," *Deseret News*, 28 February 2004.

2. "Work in Brazil 'a Miracle'; Will Grow," *Deseret News*, 28 February 2004.

3. J. M. Heslop, "Area Conference in Brazil," *Church News*, 18 August 1975, 3.

4. J. M. Heslop, "Greater Need Brings Temple's Renovation," *Church News*, 19 April 1975, 3.

5. Nelson C. Aidukaitis, "Temple Progresses in Brazil, " *Church News*, 16 January 1977, 3.

6. Ibid., 10.

A TEMPTING PROPOSITION

1. George C. Lambert, in George Q. Cannon, *Gems of Reminiscence: Faith-Promoting Series*, no. 17 (Salt Lake City: Juvenile Instructor Office, 1915), 182.

NOTES

An Inspired Site Selection

1. David Henry Cannon Jr., in Kirk M. Curtis, *History of the St. George Temple*, master's thesis, Brigham Young University. Quoted in Janice Force DeMille, *The St. George Temple—First 100 Years* (Hurricane, UT: Homestead Publishers, 1977), 20–21.

Removing the Cactus

1. Shanna Ghaznavi, "A Site to Behold," *New Era*, November 1998.

2. Tony Knudsen (temple construction missionary), interview by author, audio recording, 25 February 2000.

Altar Cloth Sisters

1. Twila Bird, *Build unto My Holy Name: The Story of the Denver Temple* (Denver: Denver Colorado Area Public Communications Council, 1987), 89.

2. Ibid., 91.

3. Ibid., 89.

From Rags to Carpet

1. Nolan P. Olsen, *Logan Temple—The First 100 Years* (Logan, UT: Keith W. Watkins and Sons Inc., 1978), 129–30.

Celestial Room Generosity

1. Weldon Smith and Doris Smith (Baton Rouge Louisiana Temple construction missionaries), interview by author, audio recording, 12 September 2000.

On the Amazon and over the Andes

1. Jason Swensen, "Faithful Peruvians Claim Temple Blessings," *Church News*, 19 May 2001.

2. Ibid.

3. Ibid.

Running Out of Marble

1. Gale Mair, interview by author, audio recording, 12 April 2000.

NOTES

"CTR" MEANS "CHOOSE THE RIGHT"

1. Leo C. Udy and Rhea Udy (Edmonton Alberta Temple construction missionaries), interview by author, audio recording, 12 May 2000.

NO LIVES WERE LOST

1. Herbert Jarvis, in N. B. Lundwall, compiler, *Temples of the Most High* (Salt Lake City: Bookcraft, 1968), 80–81.

2. Ibid.

3. Ellen Snow Ence as quoted in Janice Force DeMille, *The St. George Temple—First 100 Years* (Hurricane, UT: Homestead Publishers, 1977), 93.

INTERIOR DESIGN CHALLENGES

1. Greg E. Hill, in letter to Lubbock temple president Jay B. Jensen, 9 April 2002, used by permission.

2. Beth Pratt, "Mormons Readying Temple for Dedication," *The Lubbock Avalanche-Journal*, 23 March 2002. Also in Hill to Jensen letter, 9 April 2002.

3. Hill to Jensen letter, 9 April 2002.

4. Ibid.

THE RIGHT STONE AT THE RIGHT PRICE

1. Jean Anne Turner, compiler, "Newport Beach Temple: Plans and Approval," 1 September 2006, 6, unpublished document, copy in author's possession, used by permission.

2. Ibid.

3. Vernon Forbush, interview by author, audio recording, 3 June 2005.

A SPECIAL DEDICATORY SESSION

1. "Lima Temple Dedication Brings Blessings to Saints in Peru, Bolivia," *Ensign*, March 1986, 83.

2. Sheri L. Dew, *Go Forward with Faith: The Biography of Gordon B. Hinckley* (Salt Lake City: Deseret Book, 1996), 479.

CONVERTED WHILE BUILDING A TEMPLE

1. "Temple Superintendent Baptized," *The Raleigh Temple Times*, 2 October 1999, 2.

NOTES

2. R. Scott Lloyd, "While Building Temple, He Embraced the Gospel," *Church News*, 25 December 1999.

3. Ibid.

AN AMAZON EXODUS

1. Nelson C. Aidukaitis, "Temple Progresses in Brazil," *Church News*, 15 January 1977, 10.

2. Uilson Felipe Santiago and Linda Ritchie Archibald, "From Amazon Basin to Temple," *Church News*, 13 March 1993, 6.

LAND PRESERVED FOR A TEMPLE

1. "Ground Broken for Two New Temples," *Church News*, 17 October 1998, 3.

2. Ibid.

3. Greg Hill, "A Temple in Their Midst," *Church News*, 30 October 1999, 3.

A HOME FOR THE TEMPLE PRESIDENT

1. Jay B. Jensen (Lubbock Texas Temple's first temple president), "Lubbock Texas Temple History," talk given in sacrament meeting on 13 March 2005, copy in author's possession, used by permission.

THE MIRACLE OF THE FISHES AND LOAVES OF BREAD

1. Charles W. Allen, *Window Maker* (Nauvoo, IL: Allyn House, 2000), 177.

2. Ibid., 69.

THE LORD LOANED HIM TO US

1. Avis Laverne in Norma Baldwin Ricketts, *Arizona's Honeymoon Trail: Mormon Wagon Roads* (Mesa, AZ: Cox Printing, 2001), 127–28.

A BELL WITH A LEGACY

1. Maud Lamoreaux Card, Neil Lamoreaux Clayton, and Lulu Lamoreaux Jones, "The Nauvoo Bell," typescript received from Edith Smith Eliot, copy in possession of Lois Leetham Tanner, in "I Have a Question," *Ensign*, February 1981, 14–16.

2. B. H. Roberts, *A Comprehensive History of the Church*, 5 vol. (Salt Lake City: Deseret News Press, 1930), 5:136.

NOTES

3. "As We See It," *Church News*, 29 July 1961.

4. Stephen A. Martin, "Angels Take Their Places on 3 Temples," *Deseret News*, 22 September 2001.

FINDING PROPERTY IN HONG KONG

1. "Where the Twain Meet" (a video production), KSL Television, Salt Lake City, 1996.

2. Gordon B. Hinckley, in Dew, *Go Forward with Faith*, 481.

3. "Where the Twain Meet."

MY ANGEL MOTHER

1. In Rell G. Francis, *Cyrus E. Dallin: Let Justice Be Done* (Springville, UT: Springville Museum of Art, 1976), 66, as quoted in Richard Neitzel Holzapfel, *Every Stone a Sermon* (Salt Lake City: Bookcraft, 1992), 48–49.

2. Ibid.

3. Levi Edgar Young, "The Angel Moroni and Cyrus Dallin," *Improvement Era*, April 1953, 234.

4. J. Michael Hunter, "'I Saw Another Angel Fly'," *Liahona*, August 2000, 12.

ANCESTORS DRESSED IN WHITE

1. Anthon H. Lund, in N.B. Lundwall, comp., *Temples of the Most High* (Salt Lake City: Bookcraft, 1968), 116.

THE "MCKAY OAK" LEGACY

1. Terry Warner, "A Temple for Great Britain," *Millennial Star*, May 1958, 267.

2. "Seedlings Sprout from Ancient Oak Named in Honor of Pres. McKay," *Church News*, 2 November 1963, 3.

3. Ibid.

4. Peter Lassig, interview by author, audio recording, 30 July 2007.

A SITE OVERLOOKING THE CITY

1. Neal A. Maxwell, as quoted in Dew, *Go Forward with Faith*, 480.

2. Philippe Kradolfer, as quoted in Dew, *Go Forward with Faith*, 481.

NOTES

FINDING GREAT JOY IN GIVING

1. Weatherford T. Clayton (Newport Beach stake president), interview by author, audio recording, 3 June 2005.

2. Joseph I. Bentley (Newport Beach Temple committee chairman), interview by author, audio recording, 3 June 2005.

ONLY THE WHITEST MARBLE

1. Marvin and Karla Prestridge (Louisville Kentucky Temple construction missionaries), interview by author, audio recording, 11 March 2000.

DETERMINED TO SERVE IN THE TEMPLE

1. John L. Hart, "Temple Moments: I'm Here!" *Church News*, 5 February 1994.

A WORTHY TRADE SPECIALIST

1. Donna Jones Hessling, "Temple Moments: Another Way," *Church News*, 22 May 2004.

LIGHTNING STRIKES

1. In *Color Country Spectrum*, 13 April 1977, quoted in Janice Force DeMille, *The St. George Temple—First 100 Years* (Hurricane, UT: Homestead Publishers, 1977), 87–88.

2. Ibid.

3. Ibid.

4. As recorded in author's journal.

INDEX

INDEX

INDEX

INDEX